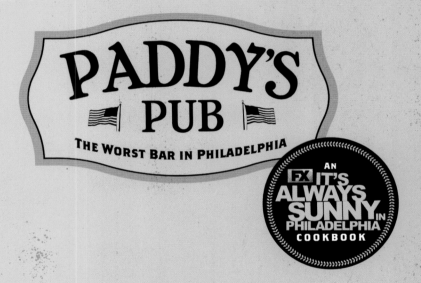

PADDY'S
PUB
THE WORST BAR IN PHILADELPHIA

AN
FX IT'S
ALWAYS
SUNNY IN
PHILADELPHIA
COOKBOOK

PADDY'S PUB

THE WORST BAR IN PHILADELPHIA

RECIPES BY
LAUREL RANDOLPH

FOOD PHOTOGRAPHY BY
NOAH FECKS

HYPERION
AVENUE

LOS ANGELES · NEW YORK

AN
FX IT'S
ALWAYS
SUNNY IN
PHILADELPHIA
COOKBOOK

First Hardcover Edition, September 2023
10 9 8 7 6 5 4 3 2 1
FAC-034274-23215
Printed in the United States of America

This book is set in Factoria, Brothers, Lobseter, and Industry Adobe fonts.

Introduction and interstitials by Ross Maloney
Food photography by Noah Fecks
Food styling by Maggie Ruggiero
Prop styling by Ethan Lunkenheimer
Cover and book design by Amy C. King
Editorial by Cassidy Leyendecker

Library of Congress Control Number: 2022952481
ISBN 978-1-368-08379-9
Reinforced binding

CONTENTS

FRANK

Dennis

MAC

DEE

A Letter from the Editor:

BEFORE YOU READ ANY FURTHER, I feel obligated to explain why this is not your typical cookbook. Consider it a disclaimer of sorts.

The purpose of this series was to highlight celebrities who cook and share their favorite recipes. Celebrity partnerships are a powerful engine in today's e-commerce landscape, and we had been trying to make a play into that market to expand sales. However, after discovering that the initial celebrities we wanted to work with were either not open to collaboration or did not cook for themselves, we made the ill-judged and continuously haunting mistake of casting too wide a net and opening up our search to online forums. This has proved to be our undoing, and now we are reaping what we have sown.

We revised our searches from A-list Hollywood celebrities to more localized regional celebs who may offer a unique culinary voice and an authentic cultural perspective. This is when we found Ronald McDonald, Dennis Reynolds, and Charlie Kelly in the comments section of a query we posted on a South Philadelphia Reddit board. They were the only comments that had received any upvotes, but by the easy math, we now see they were simply upvoting one another. Mr. Kelly's account had been active for less than a day, so we suspect the others coerced him into signing up for the site solely to contribute to this manipulation.

The three gentlemen posited that Paddy's Pub in South Philadelphia was "local celebrity-owned" and operated by "recognizable faces who have been on TV many times," but that it "would be better not to spoil the surprise and for you to come see for yourselves." They said the owners' reach went beyond Philadelphia, too, as they are venerated actors and writers who have worked with M. Night Shyamalan and appeared in the *Lethal Weapon* franchise.

Sure, you reading at home would've called malarkey and stopped there. But this project was already greenlit, and, though I'll spare you the screed on the profitability of publishing in 2023, suffice it to say when a book these days is funded, you follow any lead you get to ensure it reaches print.

Once we arrived onsite, three things became immediately apparent: First, we had been catfished. Second, the bar was, in fact, owned by Mr. McDonald, Mr. Reynolds, and Mr. Kelly, plus two more of their cohorts (Mr. Frank Reynolds, an older man who kept flaunting his wealth, and Ms. Deandra Reynolds, a woman with a gargantuan wingspan who kept flaunting her, shall we say, dated comedic impressions). And third, none of them were famous actors. Ms. Reynolds kept claiming she was, but even the core three culprits who had so deceptively lured us in fought with principle to dispel that.

At that point, however, it was too late to back out. Our flights and hotels were a sunk cost, we had promised pages to our board, and no actual celebrities had taken up our requests to interview. We had no choice but to take these five strangers on their word that they were famous in South Philly. They weren't. Not exactly. Perhaps *infamous* is a better word.

The good news is that they did provide us with a cookbook's worth of recipes. Recipes you will never find in any other book, probably out of respect for the communal well-being. But we brought in an esteemed food writer to make sure each is actually edible and a highly professional photo and design team to make these dishes, as much as I hate to say it, appetizing to a point worth trying. Because "the Gang" could not collectively agree on which recipes to share, each member has staked out a portion of the book to promote their own shortlist. And as we don't want to imply endorsement of anything herein from a philosophical standpoint, we have left it to the Gang to introduce their sections in their own words.

To anyone reading, please see this as the cautionary tale it is: of how journalists should always vet their sources, of how risky it is to take information off the Internet in good faith, and of how there is always a price to pay for compromising your intents in service of a bottom line. I'm sorry in advance to anyone from the region who feels misrepresented by these "Philly favorites." We've tried to account for it with the subtitle *The Worst Bar in Philadelphia*, but please know that if we could've stopped this sooner, we would have. If only The Rock had returned our calls . . .

"Charlie"

HELLO. I'M CHARLIE KELLY, and as a person who both reads and writes, I'm definitely typing out this section myself. Dennis is not helping me in any fashion. He's also not helping with any fashion in any fashion, because if you ask me, he doesn't understand the beauty of a good horse shirt or an extra-worn pair of tighty-whities. What? No, just put it, dude. That way they'll know it was from me. Okay, don't knock the underwear until you've tried it! I told you: the more you keep wearing it, the softer and stretchier the fabric becomes.

Anyhoo, I'll be honest that I wasn't on board with releasing some of these recipes to begin with. Not because they are well-kept family secrets or anything like that—I never knew my dad until right before he was murdered by a shrill Irish ghost-woman with COVID, and my mother was always too busy catching up with our male neighbors to cook much for me—but because they're my own thing, and sometimes it's nice just to have something for yourself and the person you share a couch with at night.

But then, Dennis and Mac convinced me that the real joy was in sharing your happiness with others—and they told me there would be some money in it for me, so I agreed. How much did you say I'd be making again? Oh, wait. That was me talking to myself. No, dude, no one knows you're here. Stop. Just keep typing what I'm saying. But how much did you say I'll get? $50?? Nice!

Alright, enjoy my section of nutritious snacks, and remember: they're always tastier on the radiator.

GRILLED CHARLIE

This fancified version of a Grilled Charlie has all the key elements—peanut butter, chocolate, butter, and cheese—and in the right order. Sliced cheese is swapped for a fluffy cream cheese frosting, turning the melty-chocolate-and-peanut-butter sandwich into a decadent dessert.

Serves 2 to 4 · Prep Time: 10 minutes · Cook Time: 6 minutes

FOR THE FROSTING:

4 ounces cream cheese, softened

2 tablespoons sugar

½ teaspoon vanilla extract

4 to 5 tablespoons heavy cream

FOR THE SANDWICH:

1 tablespoon butter, softened

4 slices brioche or challah bread

⅔ cup semisweet chocolate chips

¼ cup salted, smooth peanut butter

Chocolate sauce, for topping, optional

FRANK: *"The butter goes on and then the peanut butter. . . ."*

CHARLIE: *"Peanut butter outside, chocolate inside! Butter inside, cheese outside!"*

1. Add the softened cream cheese, sugar, and vanilla to a small mixing bowl. Beat with a hand mixer until creamy and the sugar has dissolved, about 1 minute. Add 4 tablespoons heavy cream and beat, adding up to an additional tablespoon as needed to make a fluffy, creamy frosting. Set aside.

2. Butter both sides of all 4 slices of bread. Heat a large skillet over low heat. Once warm, add two slices of bread, side by side, and top each with chocolate chips. Place the remaining slices of bread over the chocolate to make 2 sandwiches.

3. Turn the heat up to medium and cook until the bottom is golden brown and the chocolate is becoming melty, about 3 minutes. Flip and toast on the other side for 2 to 3 minutes.

4. Remove to plates and let cool for a few minutes. Spread the top of each sandwich with peanut butter. Top each with a mound of cream cheese frosting, and, if desired, drizzle with chocolate sauce. Serve warm.

Variations:

Swap the chocolate chips for chocolate-hazelnut spread.

If you don't have brioche or challah, white bread will work just fine.

CAT FOOD

While this flavorful tuna salad isn't guaranteed to help you sleep, it does make a great lunch or snack. The recipe is easy to tweak by adjusting the amount of mayo or pickle relish, or by adding extra ingredients like fresh herbs. Serve with crackers or pile onto bread to make a sandwich.

Serves 1 · Prep Time: 10 minutes · Cook Time: 0 minutes

1 (5-ounce) can chunk white tuna in water

2 to 4 tablespoons mayonnaise

2 tablespoons minced celery

1 heaping teaspoon minced onion

1 heaping teaspoon pickle relish, optional

1 lemon wedge

Salt and pepper, to taste

Fresh herbs, optional

Crackers or bread, optional

1. Open the tuna and drain, adding the tuna to a small mixing bowl. Don't discard the can.

2. Add the mayonnaise (starting with 2 tablespoons), celery, onion, and relish (if using). Squeeze the lemon wedge over top and season with salt and pepper.

3. Mix and taste for seasoning, adding more mayonnaise or salt and pepper to taste. Serve in the tuna can.

FRANK: *"Well, if I was hungry and the cat food was there, I'd eat it. And if I couldn't sleep, I'd eat the cat food because—"*

CHARLIE: *"It might make you go to sleep!"*

MAC: *"In what scenario would you not eat the cat food?"*

FRANK: *"I would always eat the cat food."*

MEAT CUBES

Nothing says thank you quite like a box of meat cubes. The key is buying quality cured meat from a good deli and having it custom sliced into thick pieces. There are tons of ways to serve meat cubes beyond placing them in an ornate box as a thank-you gift, from skewers to cheese plates to salads.

Serves 6 · Prep Time: 10 minutes · Cook Time: 0 minutes

1 to 2 pounds mortadella or salami, cut into 1-inch-thick slices

MAC: *"We're setting up a meet-cute."*

CHARLIE: *"Are you trying to say 'a meat cube,' like a little cube of meat? Because that's a good idea actually."*

1. Using a sharp chef's knife, trim the edges of the mortadella or salami to make a square. Cut the square into 1-inch cubes. Reserve the scraps for chopping and tossing into omelets, frittatas, and more.

2. Place in a box lined with parchment or waxed paper and serve.

TIP: Head to a deli for those big, fat rolls of cured meat that are sliced to order, then beg the person behind the counter to skip the meat slicer and cut them into 1-inch-thick pieces. Any cured meat available in large logs will work.

Variations:

There are plenty of fun ways to serve meat cubes. Thread them on long party toothpicks with cubes of cheese for a quick, make-ahead appetizer.

Serve meat cubes as part of a cheese platter. Mortadella and salami pair well with a variety of cheeses like mild cheddar, Brie, Manchego, Gouda, or goat cheese.

Use as a hardy topping for a chopped salad along with provolone, peperoncini, chickpeas, red onions, and tomatoes.

Stick a cube or two on a cocktail toothpick along with a gherkin and use to garnish a Bloody Mary.

SPA-DAY SPAGHETTI

This spaghetti-and-meatball recipe is ready in under 30 minutes, so it's perfect for taking on the go to the movie theater or spa (depending on their spaghetti policies). A homemade sauce makes it special, while frozen meatballs keep it quick and easy.

Serves 3 to 4 · Prep Time: 5 minutes · Cook Time: 20 minutes

2 tablespoons olive oil

4 garlic cloves, minced

1 (28-ounce) can
crushed tomatoes

1 teaspoon dried oregano
or basil

12 frozen meatballs

¾ pound spaghetti

2 tablespoons butter

Salt and pepper, to taste

Grated Parmesan, for serving

DEE: *"So I thought I would take you for a spa day, just you and me."*

CHARLIE: *"A what day?"*

DEE: *"A spa day."*

CHARLIE: *"What is this word 'spa'? I feel like you're starting to say a word and you're not finishing it. Are you trying to say 'spaghetti'? Are you taking me for a spaghetti day?"*

1. Put a large pot of salted water on to boil.

2. Heat the olive oil in a large saucepan over medium-low heat. Add the garlic and cook just until fragrant, about 30 seconds.

3. Add the crushed tomatoes and oregano or basil and stir. Bring to a low simmer, adjusting the heat as needed. Add the frozen meatballs, mostly submerging them in sauce. Let simmer for 15 minutes, stirring occasionally.

4. Meanwhile, cook the pasta until al dente according to the package directions. Reserve a cup of pasta water and drain the pasta.

5. Add the butter to the sauce and let melt. Taste the sauce, adding salt and pepper as needed.

6. Add the drained pasta and ¼ cup of pasta water to the sauce. Increase the heat to medium and stir and toss the pasta for a few minutes until it is well coated and the sauce is the right consistency. Add more pasta water if it is too dry.

7. Serve topped with Parmesan.

Variation:

You can substitute frozen meatballs for homemade. Brown them in a skillet or the oven and then add them to the sauce as directed to finish cooking through.

MILK STEAK

Charlie might like his steak boiled over hard in milk, but no one else does. For this recipe, cube steaks are coated in milk before being battered and fried like chicken, and a milk gravy adds a savory, creamy element. Serve this country-fried steak with a side of raw jelly beans.

Serves 4 · Prep Time: 15 minutes · Cook Time: 20 minutes

FOR THE STEAK:

2 pounds cube steak

2 teaspoons kosher salt, divided

¼ teaspoon black pepper, divided

1½ cups all-purpose flour

1 teaspoon paprika

1 teaspoon garlic powder

2 eggs

⅔ cup whole milk

Canola or vegetable oil, for frying

FOR THE MILK GRAVY:

2 tablespoons butter

¼ cup seasoned flour mixture, left over from above

2½ cups whole milk

Up to 1 tablespoon hot sauce, such as Tabasco, optional

1 teaspoon kosher salt, or to taste

½ teaspoon black pepper, or to taste

1. Season the steaks on both sides with 1 teaspoon kosher salt and ⅛ teaspoon pepper.

2. In a shallow bowl, combine the flour, remaining 1 teaspoon salt, remaining ⅛ teaspoon pepper, paprika, and garlic powder. Whisk together.

3. In another shallow bowl, add the eggs and milk and beat until combined.

4. Dust a steak in the flour mixture, pressing to adhere and turning to coat completely. Gently shake off any excess and place the steak in the egg mixture, turning to coat completely. Briefly let any excess drip off, then return the steak to the flour mixture. Coat completely, press to adhere, and place the breaded steak on a plate. Repeat with the remaining steaks, arranging them in a single layer. Don't discard the flour mixture.

[continued on next page]

DENNIS: *"How about your favorite food? What would that be?"*

CHARLIE: *"Oh, milk steak."*

DENNIS: *"I'm not putting milk steak. I'm gonna put steak."*

CHARLIE: *"Don't put steak. Put milk steak. She'll know what it is."*

(continued from previous page)

5. Place a large frying pan on the stove over medium heat. Add enough oil to completely cover the bottom of the pan in a thin layer—it should reach about halfway up the steaks once they are added to the pan. The oil is hot enough when you drop in a little flour and it sizzles but does not burn.

6. Add the steaks, working in batches if needed so you don't overcrowd the pan, and fry until the edges are golden brown, 2 to 3 minutes. Flip and cook until the other side is golden brown all over, 2 to 3 more minutes.

7. Transfer the steaks to a paper towel–lined platter and repeat with the remaining steaks.

8. Once all the steak has been cooked, make the gravy. Drain off all but 2 tablespoons of the oil, leaving most of the browned bits behind. Add the butter and melt.

9. Sprinkle in ¼ cup of the leftover seasoned flour that you used to bread the steak and stir, cooking until it forms a thin paste. Continue to cook and stir until it turns a caramel color, about 4 minutes.

10. Add the milk in a slow stream, whisking constantly. Add the hot sauce (if using), salt, and pepper to taste and mix. Cook until the gravy is heated through and thickened, stirring occasionally, about 5 minutes.

11. Serve the steaks immediately, topped with gravy.

CHARLIE: *"Now, I'm gonna want the milk steak. Boiled over hard. And a side of your finest jelly beans, raw."*

CREAM PIE

Get your head out of the gutter. This is an actual coconut cream pie with a luxurious custard filling and fluffy whipped cream on top. The cookie crust includes shredded coconut for extra flavor and texture, as does the fluffy top. Make the pie a day before serving so it can set properly before slicing.

Makes 1 pie · Prep Time: 30 minutes · Cook Time: 20 minutes · Chill Time: 7 hours

FOR THE COCONUT CUSTARD:

¼ cup all-purpose flour

½ cup sugar

½ teaspoon salt

1 [13- to 14-ounce] can full-fat coconut milk

½ cup whole milk

2 large eggs

2 tablespoons unsalted butter

1½ teaspoons vanilla extract

½ teaspoon coconut extract, optional

FOR THE CRUST AND WHIPPED CREAM:

35 vanilla wafer cookies [4.2 ounces]

¾ cup unsweetened coconut flakes, divided

1 tablespoon brown sugar

¼ teaspoon salt

⅓ cup unsalted butter, melted

1½ cups heavy cream

2 tablespoons sugar

½ teaspoon vanilla extract

1. To make the coconut custard, combine the flour, sugar, and salt in a medium-sized heavy-bottomed saucepan and whisk. Add the coconut milk, milk, and eggs and whisk well to thoroughly combine.

2. Place the pan over medium heat. Bring the mixture to a boil while stirring—bubbles should be popping up all over the pan, including the center. Boil, stirring constantly and scraping the bottom, for 5 full minutes.

3. Remove from the heat and add the butter, vanilla, and coconut extract (if using). Stir until the butter is melted and the custard is creamy.

4. Pour the custard into a bowl and press a piece of greased plastic wrap directly against the surface. Chill in the fridge for at least 4 hours or overnight.

5. To make the crust, preheat the oven to 350°F. Add the vanilla wafers to a food processor and pulse several times until the cookies are all broken into small pieces. Add ½ cup of coconut flakes, the brown sugar, and the salt and pulse until the cookies are finely ground.

[continued on next page]

FRANK: *"God bless cream pies and god bless America . . . and China, too."*

[continued from previous page]

6. Add the melted butter and stir with a rubber spatula until all the crumbs are saturated. Pour the mixture into a 9-inch pie pan and press against the bottom and sides, creating an even, well-packed layer.

7. Bake until golden brown and fragrant, about 10 minutes. Let cool completely.

8. If desired, toast the remaining ¼ cup coconut flakes in a pan over medium heat until golden brown. Let cool.

9. To make the whipped cream, add the cream to a mixing bowl and beat with the whisk attachment or an electric mixer on medium-high speed until it begins to thicken. Add the sugar slowly while mixing, followed by the vanilla. Beat until stiff peaks form, being careful not to overbeat.

10. Add the chilled custard to the cooled piecrust and smooth the top. Add the whipped cream and smooth with a spatula. Chill, uncovered, for at least 3 hours or up to 24 hours. Top with coconut flakes before serving.

Variation:

Instead of a homemade coconut cookie crust, use a premade piecrust topped with toasted coconut.

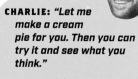

CHARLIE: *"Let me make a cream pie for you. Then you can try it and see what you think."*

DENNIS: *"I do not want to taste your cream pie."*

CHARLIE: *"They taste great. I can guarantee it."*

ENERGY BALLS

These protein-packed balls will give you the energy to conquer enemies and expand your virtual kingdom. They taste remarkably like peanut butter cookie dough and keep in the fridge for a week, making them a handy anytime snack.

Makes 30 to 35 balls · Prep Time: 20 minutes · Cook Time: 0 minutes · Chill Time: 1 hour

1 cup rolled oats or 1 cup plus 1 tablespoon oat flour

1 cup creamy natural peanut butter, stirred

¼ cup honey

2 tablespoons vanilla protein powder

1 to 3 tablespoons milk or nondairy milk

Pinch of salt

CHARLIE: *"To sustain me."*

1. Pour the rolled oats into a small food processor, high-speed blender, or spice grinder and process into a fine powder. Alternatively, use oat flour.

2. Transfer the powdered oats or oat flour to a medium-sized bowl and add the peanut butter, honey, protein powder, 1 tablespoon milk, and salt.

3. Use a wooden spoon or rubber spatula to mix until a dough forms. Add more milk as needed to make a mixture with the consistency of thick cookie dough.

4. Form the mixture into 1-inch balls with your hands. Chill for at least 1 hour, then store in a container in the fridge.

Variations:

Swap the protein powder for the same amount of ground flaxseed or more oat flour plus ½ teaspoon vanilla extract.

Add ⅓ cup mini chocolate chips or crushed peanuts for texture.

WADE BOGGS CHICKEN

While store-bought rotisserie chickens are convenient, this homemade version is superior in flavor and texture. For a super-moist, tender bird, add chicken broth to the pan and cover for most of the cook time. It's finished uncovered at a high temperature to crisp the skin before serving.

Makes 1 whole chicken · Prep Time: 10 minutes · Cook Time: 90 minutes

1 [4- to 5-pound] whole chicken, giblets removed

1 tablespoon kosher salt

1½ teaspoons smoked paprika

½ teaspoon black pepper

½ teaspoon garlic powder

½ teaspoon onion powder

½ teaspoon dried thyme

2 tablespoons olive oil

1 lemon, halved

1 cup chicken broth

1. Preheat the oven to 350°F. Pat the chicken dry inside and out with paper towels and add to a roasting pan or 4-quart baking dish.

2. In a small bowl, combine the salt, paprika, pepper, garlic powder, onion powder, and thyme and mix.

3. Rub the chicken all over with olive oil. Rub the inside and outside of the chicken with the seasoning mix. Place the halved lemon inside the cavity.

4. Add the chicken broth to the pan around the chicken. Cover the pan tightly with aluminum foil and bake until the chicken reaches 140°F, 1 to 1½ hours.

5. Remove the chicken from the oven and increase the oven temperature to 450°F. Remove the foil and baste the chicken with the pan juices before returning it to the oven (it's okay if the oven hasn't reached 450°F yet).

6. Roast until the chicken registers at least 165°F in the thickest parts without hitting a bone, the juices run clear, and the skin is crisp, 20 to 30 minutes.

7. Let the chicken sit, uncovered, for 10 minutes before carving.

MAC: *"Why are you filling up on chicken?"*

CHARLIE: *"Do you know anything about Wade Boggs? The man ate a chicken before every game! That's why they call him the Chicken Man."*

CHARLIE'S RICE KRISPIES TREATS

Rice Krispies treats are one of the most beloved snackable desserts, and for good reason. They require only three ingredients, they're quick and easy, and they're tasty. This take on the classic can be made with your choice of cereal (or a mix of cereals!) and is sure to ward off any cranky landlords.

Makes 12 to 16 bars · Prep Time: 10 minutes · Cook Time: 10 minutes

½ cup salted butter

1 (10-ounce) bag mini marshmallows

6 to 7 cups cereal

1. Grease a 9 x 9-inch inch pan and a rubber spatula and set aside.

2. Melt the butter in a large pot over medium-low heat. Add the marshmallows and stir until melted.

3. Remove the pot from the heat and add the cereal. Use 6 cups of really small cereal, like Rice Krispies, or use 7 cups of slightly bigger cereal, like Froot Loops. Stir to coat completely.

4. Dump the mixture into the prepared pan. Use the rubber spatula to gently press into the pan to make an even layer.

5. Let cool completely. Grease a sharp knife cut into squares, and serve.

TIP: Choose a cereal or cereals with smaller components for the best treats. Brands that work well include Rice Krispies, Cheerios of any kind, Fruity Pebbles, Cocoa Pebbles, Lucky Charms, Kix, Apple Jacks, Froot Loops, and Cocoa Krispies.

CHARLIE: *"I've got some Rice Krispie treats in the fridge, you want some more of those?"*

SQUASHED BEEF

If you're looking to squash some beef, then invite over your nemesis for this meal. The roast beef and winter squash are roasted at the same time for easy multitasking. Slice the roast beef super thin and use the cold leftovers to make sandwiches.

Serves 6 · Prep Time: 20 minutes · Cook Time: 2½ hours

Bringing Roast to Room Temp: 1 hour

1 (2- to 3-pound) boneless rump roast

1½ to 2 teaspoons kosher salt, divided

1 butternut squash (about 3 pounds)

2 tablespoons olive oil, divided

2 to 3 tablespoons sour cream

2 tablespoons unsalted butter, room temperature, cubed

2 to 3 teaspoons maple syrup, to taste

¼ teaspoon black pepper

1. Remove the rump roast from the fridge 1 hour before cooking. Season all over with 1 to 1½ teaspoons salt (depending on the size of your roast).

2. Meanwhile, cut the butternut squash in half lengthwise and remove the seeds. Coat with 1 tablespoon of olive oil and place, cut side down, on a rimmed baking sheet lined with foil.

3. Position an oven rack in the top third of the oven and another in the bottom third. Preheat the oven to 400°F. Rub the roast with the remaining 1 tablespoon of olive oil. Place a wire rack inside a rimmed baking sheet and place the roast on top, fat side facing up.

4. Slide the roast to the top oven rack and the butternut squash to the bottom rack. Bake for 20 minutes or until the roast is browned. Reduce the oven temperature to 275°F without opening the oven door.

5. Check the butternut squash 30 minutes after reducing the temperature, then check every 10 minutes as needed. It's ready when you can very easily insert a paring knife into the thickest part. Once the squash is done cooking, remove it from the oven and leave the roast in the oven.

(continued on next page)

(continued from previous page)

6. Using a meat thermometer, check the roast 1½ hours after reducing the temperature. The internal temperature should read 145°F for medium doneness. If the roast isn't done, check again every 20 or so minutes. Depending on your oven and the cut of beef, it will take a smaller roast as little as 1½ hours and a larger roast up to 3½ hours after reducing the temperature to finish cooking. Once done, remove the pan from the oven and tent the roast with aluminum foil. Let rest for 20 minutes.

7. Meanwhile, let the squash cool enough to handle, and then scoop the flesh from the peel; add it to a medium-sized mixing bowl. Add the sour cream, butter, maple syrup, ½ teaspoon salt, and pepper and mash using a potato masher. Adjust the seasoning based on the size of the squash and to taste. Cover tightly.

8. Once the roast has rested, place it on a cutting board and use a sharp serrated or chef's knife to cut it against the grain into very thin slices. If needed, reheat the mashed butternut squash in 30-second intervals in the microwave. Serve.

TIP: Roast beef is good with gravy. You can make a homemade gravy using the pan drippings or serve with store-bought.

Both the beef and the squash are good made ahead of time. Reheat the squash in the oven or microwave and wait to slice the beef until serving time.

DENNIS: *"So we're literally serving squash and beef?"*

CHARLIE: *"I thought it would be part of the ceremony to have squash and beef!"*

The Waitress's Cherry Pie

Boozy with just the right balance of sweet and tart, this cherry pie is, thankfully, lacking a key ingredient: poison. The bourbon adds a caramelized, slightly smoky flavor that goes incredibly well with the fruit and pastry. Serve with vanilla ice cream or whipped cream.

Makes 1 pie · Prep Time: 30 minutes · Cook Time: 50 minutes

- ¾ cup sugar, plus more for sprinkling on the crust
- ¼ cup cornstarch
- ½ teaspoon salt
- 2 (14- to 15-ounce) cans sour cherries in water, drained
- 1 (15-ounce) can sweet cherries in light syrup, drained, with ¼ cup of syrup reserved
- ¼ cup bourbon
- 1 teaspoon vanilla extract
- ¼ teaspoon almond extract
- 2 store-bought refrigerated piecrusts
- 1 egg, beaten with 1 tablespoon water
- Vanilla ice cream or whipped cream, for serving

Variation:

You can make this pie using all canned sweet cherries. Reduce the sugar to ½ cup and add 1 tablespoon of lemon juice along with the vanilla and almond extracts.

1. Position an oven rack in the bottom third of the oven and preheat oven to 425°F. Line a rimmed baking sheet with foil.

2. Add the sugar, cornstarch, and salt to a medium-sized saucepan and whisk together. Add the drained sour and sweet cherries, reserved syrup, and bourbon and stir to combine using a wooden spoon or rubber spatula.

3. Heat over medium heat, stirring often, until the mixture is bubbly throughout and has thickened. Remove from the heat and stir in the vanilla and almond extracts. Let cool for at least 10 minutes.

4. Line a 9-inch pie plate with one piecrust, folding any excess dough under around the edge. Add the pie filling to the crust, smoothing the top. Paint the edge of the crust with the egg wash and transfer the pie dish to the lined baking sheet.

5. Unroll the second piecrust on a clean surface and use a pizza cutter or sharp knife to slice it into 1-inch strips. Use the strips to form a lattice crust on top of the pie, and press the ends into the edges of the bottom crust to adhere. Trim any excess.

6. Paint the crust lightly with the egg wash and sprinkle with sugar. Transfer the baking sheet and pie into the oven and bake until the crust is browned and the filling is bubbly, 40 to 45 minutes. If the crust is browning too much, cover the edges with foil partway through baking.

7. Let cool completely before serving with ice cream or whipped cream.

WAITRESS: *"I poisoned the pie. So you should stop eating it."*

CHARLIE: *"Last bite!"*

"Frank"

LISTEN HERE. This number you sent me is an insult. I ain't givin' up the goods for peanuts. I know how publishing works. I owned a few boutiques back in the day. Maybe yours. What'd you say your name was? Hysteria? Hyperion? Nah. Doesn't ring a bell. I was more in the game of printing holy scriptures and textbooks. And in some states, they were one and the same. Helped me keep a whole lot tucked from Uncle Sam, I'll tell you that much. Then classrooms went digital, and the whole operation went belly-up. Not the holy books, though. They'll keep slicing down trees just fine. Some of my biggest customers still to date.

What I'm saying is I know my way around a markup. And just because my colleagues are eager to get their book published don't mean they're suckers. Except Mac. He is kind of a sucker. And I don't mean that about his pastimes or nothin'. He's a sweetheart, he's just kinda dim. So, I'm here to be the muscle.

How 'bout this? You give me this plus 50 percent, and I'll give you the pocket sausages you want so badly. I saw how your eyes lit up when you watched me eating them. Yeah. I saw that look. You were impressed with how much grease I wasn't getting on my fingers. Well, let's cut a deal, and your readers can be impressed with it, too.

It ain't personal, it's just business. You can tell your board that's coming straight from The Warthog. They'll know who.

PICKLED EGGS

It's important to always keep your bunker stocked with plenty of Pickled Eggs. They're easy to make and especially good served with beer. For the best flavor, let them sit in the fridge for a few days or longer before enjoying.

Serves 6 · Prep Time: 10 minutes · Cook Time: 15 minutes · Pickling Time: 3 days

6 large eggs

1 cup white or apple cider vinegar

¾ cup water

¼ cup sugar

1 garlic clove, smashed

1 teaspoon mustard seeds

½ teaspoon kosher or sea salt

3 fresh dill fronds

FRANK: "Can I offer you a nice egg in this trying time?"

1. Add about an inch of water to a steamer pot or saucepan and top with a steamer basket. Cover and bring to a boil. Meanwhile, add ice and cold water to a medium-sized mixing bowl to make an ice bath and set aside.

2. Once the water is boiling, add the eggs to the steamer basket in a single layer and cover. Steam for 12 to 15 minutes, depending on the size of your eggs and how firm you like your egg yolks.

3. Transfer the cooked eggs to the ice bath and let sit until cool enough to handle. Peel the eggs.

4. Combine the vinegar, water, sugar, garlic, mustard seeds, and salt in a small saucepan over medium heat. Bring to a boil and stir until the sugar and salt dissolve. Remove from the heat and let cool for a few minutes.

5. Add a dill frond and 2 cooked, peeled eggs to a quart-sized jar. Repeat, adding all the eggs and dill. Top with the brine and screw on the lid.

6. Transfer the eggs to the fridge and wait at least a few days, or ideally a week, before enjoying.

RUM HAM

Rum, along with brown sugar and Dijon mustard, adds a spiced, sweet flavor to glazed ham. You'll want to carry this ham—with its pineapple ring eyes and maraschino nose—everywhere you go.

Serves 12 to 14 · Prep Time: 15 minutes · Cook Time: 2½ hours

Bringing Ham to Room Temp: 30 minutes

1 (10-pound) bone-in, spiral-cut cooked ham

1½ cups brown sugar, packed

⅓ cup dark rum

2 tablespoons Dijon mustard

⅛ teaspoon ground cloves

2 pineapple rings

1 maraschino cherry

1. Remove the ham from the fridge and let sit at room temperature for 30 minutes to 1 hour. Preheat the oven to 325°F.

2. Unwrap the ham and place it cut side down on a roasting rack inside a roasting pan. Cover with aluminum foil and bake until the internal temperature registers 135°F, about 2 hours.

3. To make the glaze, combine the brown sugar, rum, mustard, and cloves in a bowl. Whisk until well combined.

4. Remove the foil from the ham, and increase the oven temperature to 375°F. Brush the ham with half the glaze. Bake, uncovered, for 15 minutes. Brush on the rest of the glaze and bake the ham until shiny and the internal temperature registers at least 145°F, 10 to 15 minutes.

5. Let rest for 10 minutes. Position two pineapple rings as eyes (securing with toothpicks, if needed) and a maraschino cherry as a nose. Serve.

FRANK: *"This is ham soaked in rum! It's loaded with booze."*

MAC: *"Goddammit, Frank, eating your drinks? That is genius!"*

GRILLED FRANK

Savory and a little sweet, there's nothing quite like a Grilled Frank.
The pancakes are a bit thinner and larger than your typical breakfast
flapjack, making them easy to wrap around your choice of meats.
Slather with pepper jelly, and stuff with bacon, sausage, and/or Spam.

4 servings · Prep Time: 20 minutes · Cook Time: 20 minutes

1 cup all-purpose flour

1 teaspoon sugar

¾ teaspoon baking powder

¼ teaspoon salt

1 to 1¼ cups whole milk

1 tablespoon oil

1 egg, beaten

2 tablespoons butter, divided

¼ cup pepper jelly

4 to 8 slices bacon, cooked until crisp

4 breakfast sausage links, cooked

4 slices Spam

1. Add the flour, sugar, baking powder, and salt to a medium-sized mixing bowl and whisk with a fork.

2. Then add 1 cup of milk, oil, and egg and whisk just until combined (some lumps are okay). The consistency should be a thin pancake batter, a little thicker than buttermilk. If needed, add more milk a tablespoon at a time, but don't overmix.

3. Heat a large nonstick skillet over medium heat. Once hot, add ½ tablespoon of butter and let melt. Tilt to coat the pan.

4. Add ⅓ cup of batter to the center of the pan. This should form roughly a 6-inch pancake. If needed, you can adjust the consistency of the batter by adding a bit more milk. If it's too thin, note that it will thicken as it sits, or you can add a touch more flour.

5. Cook until set around the edges, some bubbles are popping in the center, and the bottom is browned, 2 to 3 minutes. Flip and cook until cooked through, about 2 minutes.

6. Repeat with the remaining batter to make 3 more pancakes, adjusting the heat as needed.

7. Spread one side of each pancake with a tablespoon of pepper jelly. Place the 2 to 3 slices of cooked bacon, a sausage link, and/or a slice of Spam in the center of each pancake and roll up like a crepe. If desired, use a toothpick to secure. Serve.

CHARLIE: *"I got a pipin'-hot Grilled Frank for ya! I got the sausage, the Spam, the bacon. I got it wrapped in a jelly pancake and cooked with a stick of butter."*

FRANK: *"I don't want that, Charlie! I'm trying to get in shape!"*

CHICKEN PART SANDWICHES

Whether you're making them on your hot plate or on your stove, Chicken Part Sandwiches are sure to please. A homemade teriyaki sauce adds tons of flavor to the chicken and some moisture to the sandwich itself. Feel free to add other toppings like pickles or slaw.

Serves 6 · Prep Time: 10 minutes · Cook Time: 15 minutes · Marinate Time: 1 hour

½ cup soy sauce

⅓ cup brown sugar, packed

¼ cup pineapple juice

1 tablespoon rice vinegar

1 tablespoon grated ginger

2 garlic cloves, grated

1½ to 2 pounds boneless, skinless chicken thighs

1 tablespoon cornstarch

⅓ cup plus 1 tablespoon water, divided

2 teaspoons neutral oil (like canola oil)

6 hamburger buns

FRANK: *"I'm working on the chicken parts here. Take the buns off the radiator."*

1. Add the soy sauce, brown sugar, pineapple juice, rice vinegar, ginger, and garlic to a microwave-safe bowl. Whisk together and microwave in 30-second increments, stirring each time, just until the sugar is dissolved. Let cool for a few minutes.

2. Cut the chicken thighs into large pieces. Add them to a zip-top bag along with the cooled teriyaki sauce. Press out the air and seal, coating the chicken in the sauce. Place in the fridge and marinate for 1 hour.

3. Remove the chicken to a plate and add the sauce to a small saucepan. Whisk together the cornstarch and 1 tablespoon water in a small bowl.

4. Add ⅓ cup water to the sauce and bring to a simmer over medium heat. Add the cornstarch mixture and stir. Let simmer until thickened, 1 to 2 minutes. Turn off the heat.

5. Heat a large cast-iron or nonstick skillet over medium-high heat. Once the pan is hot, add the oil and tilt the pan to coat. Add the chicken in a single layer (working in batches if needed) and cook until opaque around the edges and browned on the bottom, 4 to 5 minutes. Flip and reduce the heat to medium. Cook until the chicken is browned on the bottom and cooked through, about 4 minutes.

6. Meanwhile, toast the buns lightly in a toaster oven or under the broiler. Toss the chicken in the teriyaki sauce and serve on the buns.

SOUP FOR POP-POP

This vegetable soup is quick, easy, and flavorful (unless you let it sit out for weeks). White beans and potatoes turn it into a meal, and you can add cooked sausage for extra flavor and protein. A sprinkle of Parmesan on top won't hurt, either.

Serves 3 to 4 · Prep Time: 10 minutes · Cook Time: 18 minutes

1 tablespoon olive oil

1 small yellow onion, chopped

2 ribs celery, chopped

1 large carrot, chopped

2 cloves garlic, minced

1 tablespoon tomato paste

½ pound white or yellow potatoes, cut into ½-inch cubes

1 can white beans, drained but not rinsed

32 ounces (4 cups) low-sodium vegetable or chicken broth

1 teaspoon kosher salt, or to taste

¼ to ½ teaspoon red pepper flakes, to taste

3 cups fresh baby spinach, packed

¼ cup chopped parsley leaves

1 tablespoon fresh lemon juice

1. Heat a large soup pot over medium heat. Add the olive oil, followed by the onion, celery, and carrot. Sauté until the onion begins to turn translucent, 4 to 5 minutes.

2. Add the garlic and tomato paste and sauté for 1 minute. Add the potatoes and white beans, then add the chicken broth. Season with salt and red pepper flakes and stir.

3. Increase the heat to medium-high and bring to a simmer. Reduce the heat to maintain a simmer and cook, uncovered, until the potatoes are fork-tender but not mushy, 10 to 12 minutes.

4. Add the spinach, parsley, and lemon juice. Stir and turn off the heat, letting it sit for a minute or two until the spinach has wilted. Taste for seasoning and serve.

Variations:

Add up to ½ pound of cooked, crumbled sausage.

Add a handful of additional chopped herbs like basil or oregano.

CHARLIE: *"See, this is why we work well together. You see free soup and you make a decision to eat it."*

MAC: *"It's horrible."*

CHARLIE: *"It's terrible soup, but we've got to stick with our decisions, right?"*

MAC: *"Yeah, can't go back on it now."*

DELAWARE RIVER GRILLED CATFISH

Whether you grew up eating local catfish or not, it's a mild, flaky fish that's perfectly suited to a high-heat grill. A simple seasoning of salt, pepper, and lemon zest gives the catfish plenty of flavor without overwhelming it. Serve with lemon wedges for squeezing over the top.

Serves 4 · Prep Time: 15 minutes · Cook Time: 6 minutes

4 medium-sized catfish fillets (1½ to 2 pounds total)

1 tablespoon olive oil

1 teaspoon kosher salt

½ teaspoon freshly ground black pepper

1 lemon, zested and cut into wedges

Canola or vegetable oil, for oiling the grates

1. Heat a grill to medium-high heat. Clean the grill grates really well.

2. Coat the catfish fillets in the olive oil. In a small bowl, combine the salt, pepper, and lemon zest. Rub the lemon zest into the salt and pepper until well distributed and fragrant.

3. Sprinkle the catfish all over with the spice mixture, pressing into the fillets to adhere.

4. Lightly oil the grill grates. Add the fillets in a single layer and cook, covered, until the fish releases from the grill, 3 to 4 minutes.

5. Carefully flip the fish and cook, uncovered, just until cooked through, 2 to 3 minutes. Remove from the grill and serve with fresh lemon wedges.

FRANK: *"You know what I'm looking forward to? Catching me some Delaware River catfish. They are so tasty! I used to eat them as a kid."*

CHARLIE: *"They're delicious! And you can taste that sort of endangered tang."*

BLUE

Build up your strength with a blue smoothie bowl. The fruity, creamy mixture is made with frozen banana, tropical fruit, and yogurt. It gets its vibrant color from blue spirulina, which you can find at health food stores and online.

Serves 2 · Prep Time: 10 minutes · Cook Time: 0 minutes

¼ to ¾ cup orange juice or milk, as needed

2 frozen ripe bananas, broken into pieces

1 cup frozen pineapple

1 cup frozen mango

⅔ cup plain or vanilla Greek yogurt

2 tablespoons nut butter

1 teaspoon blue spirulina

⅔ cup blueberries, for topping

1. Add ¼ cup of milk or orange juice to the blender followed by the bananas, pineapple, mango, yogurt, nut butter, and spirulina. Blend until thick and very smooth, adding orange juice or milk as needed to make a thick, smooth mixture.

2. Pour into 2 bowls and garnish with blueberries.

FRANK: *"Blue has the most antioxygens."*

FRANK'S SAUSAGE POCKET

While you could just stick a bunch of sausages in your shirt pocket, this pigs-in-a-blanket-style recipe is more delicious and decidedly less gross. Precooked link sausage from the store or sausages that you cook at home both work for this recipe.

Serves 2 to 4 · Prep Time: 15 minutes · Cook Time: 15 minutes

4 fully cooked link sausages, such as bratwursts

1 (8-ounce) can crescent rolls

Grainy mustard, for serving

1. Preheat the oven to 375°F. Line a rimmed baking sheet with aluminum foil.

2. Retrieve two triangles of crescent roll dough that are still attached (making a rectangle). Position the rectangle near the top corner of the baking sheet, with the long end of the dough running parallel with the top edge of the pan. Take another rectangle of dough and slightly overlap it over the bottom (longer side) of the first rectangle. Pinch and smooth the dough together, making a larger rectangle. The dough should look similar to a sheet of paper in front of you, and the shorter sides of the rectangle should be parallel with the top and bottom of the pan. Smooth any seams.

3. Position two sausages vertically and side by side at the top of the rectangle, about 1 inch apart. Fold the bottom of the pastry up and over the bottom portion of the sausages, making a pocket. Fold in about ½ inch of the edge along the left and right sides, pressing to adhere. Repeat with the remaining crescent roll dough and sausages.

4. Bake until the pastry is browned, about 15 minutes. Serve with mustard.

DENNIS: *"You have four sausage links in your pockets right now!"*

FRANK: *"Yeah, but I don't touch the sausage links. Why should I do that when I can let my shirt do the work?"*

ARTEMIS'S COBB SALAD

This recipe isn't a weird sex thing. It's just a classic Cobb salad recipe with chicken, avocado, blue cheese, and bacon. The simple vinaigrette is extremely versatile and works with just about any salad—you can double or triple it if you'd like leftovers to use throughout the week.

Serves 4 · Prep Time: 20 minutes · Cook Time: 5 minutes

FOR THE DRESSING:

3 tablespoons olive oil

2 tablespoons red wine vinegar

1 tablespoon fresh lemon juice

2 teaspoons Dijon mustard

1 teaspoon honey

½ teaspoon kosher salt

¼ teaspoon pepper

FOR THE SALAD:

3 medium-sized boneless, skinless chicken breasts

2 teaspoons olive oil

¾ teaspoon kosher salt

2 heads romaine or butter lettuce, torn

1 heaping cup grape or cherry tomatoes, halved

3 hard-boiled eggs, peeled and sliced or roughly chopped

2 ripe avocados, sliced

½ cup crumbled blue cheese

6 slices crisp-cooked and crumbled bacon or ¼ cup bacon bits

1. To make the dressing, combine the olive oil, red wine vinegar, lemon juice, mustard, honey, salt, and pepper in a small jar. Screw on the lid and shake until the honey dissolves and the dressing is well combined, about 30 seconds.

2. Use a meat mallet or rolling pin to pound the chicken to an even ½-inch thickness. Coat with the oil and season with salt.

3. Heat a large cast-iron skillet or grill pan over medium-high heat. Add the chicken and cook until browned on the bottom and releasing from the skillet, 2 to 3 minutes. Flip and cook until cooked through, 2 to 3 minutes. If needed, work in batches. Set aside to cool a bit before slicing.

4. Toss the lettuce with half the dressing and arrange it on a platter.

5. Top with mounds of tomatoes, eggs, avocado, and blue cheese. Slice the chicken and arrange it on top. Drizzle the remaining dressing over everything and sprinkle the bacon over top.

FRANK: *"Do you have any bacon bits? We like to put them in Artemis's hair and they rain down on me while we bang."*

ARTEMIS: *"I feel like a Cobb salad. It's amazing."*

"Dennis"

WELL, DEAR READER, if you've made it this far in the book, congrats. I know some of those earlier bits were a test on your sanity, and I'm not going to lie to you, some of what's to come is even worse. But here you are now, safe in the eye of the storm: the rational, emotionless center where genuine taste and sophistication can be celebrated by people who don't eat food out of garbage cans and actually know what a sea urchin is. And because I know you're wondering: yes, I lobbied them extensively to let me write all of the sections in order to be smart and play it right down the middle, but they accused me of "gatekeeping" and "not taking no for an answer." I said, well, it's our cookbook, pal, at least let me write the recipes, to which they said they "were good" and "had a real writer" for those. How 'bout that? Apparently, a collection of erotic memoirs doesn't count as "real writing" these days. Funny—now who's gatekeeping?

Just so you know, my Yelp review of Guigino's got an abundance of "Cools" and "Usefuls," so I am very qualified to speak on these. And I'll let the work here demonstrate its own value. You'll see who has the superior palate once you read this section. And just as an added precaution, I did do a pass on everyone else's sections behind their backs so they're not too savage or moronic.

Also, if Charlie asks, we're all only making $50 a pop off this thing. Got it? Oh, actually, don't mention we're making any money at all off of it to Dee. We cut her out completely.

CARMINE'S STEAK

Instead of burning steak to a crisp on the radiator, cook it the right way. Seared in a cast-iron skillet and then basted with butter until perfectly done, this is a true steakhouse-style steak in your very own home.

Serves 1 to 2 · Prep Time: 10 minutes · Cook Time: 8 minutes

Bringing Steak to Room Temp: 30 minutes

1 [12-ounce] NY strip steak, about 1 inch thick

1 teaspoon canola oil

¾ teaspoon kosher salt

2 tablespoons butter

2 garlic cloves, smashed and peeled

½ teaspoon coarsely ground pepper

DENNIS: *"Carmine's: The Place for Steaks."*

TRUCK DRIVER: *"This is the worst restaurant I've ever been to."*

1. Remove the steak from the fridge and let it reach room temperature, about 30 minutes.

2. Heat a medium-sized cast-iron skillet over high heat until just beginning to smoke, 3 to 5 minutes. Meanwhile, pat the steak dry on both sides, rub all over with oil, and season with the salt.

3. Add the steak to the pan and let sear, without moving, until browned with a good crust on the bottom, 2 to 3 minutes. Flip and repeat on the other side, about 2 minutes.

4. Reduce the heat to medium-high and add the butter and garlic. Hold the handle of the skillet with a potholder and tilt it slightly so you can scoop up the butter mix with a spoon. Use it to baste the steak a few times every 30 seconds or so, letting the skillet sit flat in between.

5. Start checking the steak for doneness after 2 minutes. For rare, remove the steak once it registers 125°F; medium-rare, 130°F to 135°F; and medium, 140°F.

6. Remove the steak to a plate, sprinkle with the pepper, and tent with foil for 10 minutes. Serve.

$8 MIMOSAS

There's no need to drink and dash when you make mimosas at home. This batch recipe is enough for six brunch guests (or one Charlie) and costs a fraction of the price. A little triple sec highlights all the citrus flavors.

Serves 6 · Prep Time: 15 minutes · Cook Time: 0 minutes

1½ cups freshly squeezed Valencia or navel orange juice

¼ cup freshly squeezed blood orange or grapefruit juice

¼ cup freshly squeezed tangerine or mandarin juice

¼ cup triple sec

1 (750-milliliter) bottle sparkling wine such as cava, prosecco, or champagne

1. Combine the orange juice, blood orange or grapefruit juice, tangerine juice, and triple sec in a large pitcher. Refrigerate until ready to serve.

2. Just before serving, add the sparkling wine, stir gently, and serve. Alternatively, fill each flute or glass ⅓ full with the juice mixture, then top with the sparkling wine.

TIP: Use whatever combination of orange, blood orange, tangerine, mandarin, and/or grapefruit juice that you like. If using grapefruit juice, use no more than ¼ cup.

MAC: *"Those mimosas were, like, eight bucks a pop, Charlie! You had, like, seven of them."*

DENNIS: *"Bro, I'm not paying for your mimosas."*

FRIENDSHIP PRAWN SALAD

Seal your friendship with a round of prawn salad. The creamy but still-light dressing pairs incredibly well with the sautéed prawns, avocado, and Parmesan. If you can't find prawns, look for the biggest shrimp you can find. "Colossal" is the largest designation (one step above jumbo), with about 12 to 15 per pound.

Serves 4 · Prep Time: 15 minutes · Cook Time: 4 minutes

¼ cup mayonnaise

3 tablespoons lemon juice

2 tablespoons olive oil

1 garlic clove, finely grated

½ teaspoon lemon zest

½ teaspoon Dijon mustard

½ teaspoon kosher salt, divided

½ teaspoon pepper, divided

2 tablespoons butter

12 colossal shrimp or medium-sized prawns (about 1 pound), peeled, deveined, and tail on

2 large heads romaine lettuce, torn

2 medium-sized ripe avocados

¼ cup grated Parmesan cheese

1. In a large mixing bowl, combine the mayonnaise, lemon juice, olive oil, garlic, lemon zest, and mustard. Season with half the salt and pepper. Whisk thoroughly to combine and set aside.

2. Add the butter to a large skillet over medium-high heat. Once melted, add the shrimp in a single layer. Cook for about 2 minutes, or until pink on the bottom. Flip and season with the remaining salt and pepper. Cook until opaque and just cooked through, about 2 more minutes. Transfer to a plate.

3. Add the romaine lettuce to the mixing bowl with the dressing and toss to coat evenly. Divide among 4 shallow bowls or salad plates. Slice the avocados and arrange on top of the lettuce in each bowl. Sprinkle with the cheese.

4. Place a few shrimp on top of the avocado in each bowl and serve.

TIP: You can use smaller shrimp, just decrease the cooking time accordingly to avoid overcooking.

FRANK: *"That is a humongous shrimp."*

DENNIS: *"That's because it's not a shrimp, Frank. It's a prawn."*

MAC: *"And I don't like prawns, so I eat around them."*

Cookies to Catch a Serial Killer

If you're looking to entrap a friend who may or may not be a serial killer, set out a pitcher of iced tea and these peanut butter–oatmeal cookies. Or make a batch simply because they're delicious, studded with white chocolate, raisins, and nuts.

Makes 18 to 20 cookies · Prep Time: 10 minutes · Cook Time: 24 minutes

¾ cup all-purpose flour

½ teaspoon baking powder

½ teaspoon salt

⅔ cup light brown sugar, packed

½ cup unsalted butter, softened

½ cup smooth peanut butter (no-stir)

1 large egg

1 teaspoon vanilla extract

¾ cup quick oats

⅓ cup white chocolate chips

⅓ cup raisins

⅓ cup peanuts or macadamia nuts, roughly chopped

DEE: *"I made you some cookies! I'm just in here changing into my bikini."*

1. Preheat the oven to 375°F and line a large baking sheet with parchment.

2. In a small mixing bowl, whisk together the flour, baking powder, and salt. Set aside.

3. In a separate medium-sized bowl, beat together the brown sugar, butter, and peanut butter with an electric mixer until fluffy and creamy, about 2 minutes. Add the egg and vanilla and beat until well combined.

4. Add the flour mixture to the butter mixture and combine. Use a wooden spoon or rubber spatula to fold in the oats, chocolate chips, raisins, and nuts.

5. Shape the dough using a 2-tablespoon cookie scoop, placing the dough at least 2 inches apart on the baking sheet. Flatten with your hand to make each mound of dough roughly 2 inches wide.

6. Bake for 11 to 14 minutes, or until lightly browned around the edges and set in the center. Let cool on the baking sheet for several minutes before transferring to a cooling rack. Repeat with the remaining dough.

Variation:

Make these peanut butter and chocolate cookies by swapping the white chocolate chips and raisins for semisweet chocolate chips.

FANCY GIN COCKTAIL

Worthy of a fancy gin bar, this take on the gin fizz is pretentious, but that's exactly how Dennis likes it. The rosemary-infused salty simple syrup will keep for weeks in the fridge and works well in just about any gin drink.

Makes 1 cocktail · Prep Time: 10 minutes · Cook Time: 0 minutes

FOR THE ROSEMARY SALTY SIMPLE SYRUP:

½ cup sugar

¼ cup water

1 teaspoon fine sea salt

1 sprig fresh rosemary

FOR THE COCKTAIL:

2 ounces London-style dry gin

¾ ounce non-pasteurized egg white

¾ ounce fresh red grapefruit juice

½ ounce fresh lemon juice

½ ounce rosemary salty simple syrup

½ to 1 ounce club soda, optional

1 dash Angostura bitters, for garnish

1 grapefruit or lemon twist, for garnish

1 sprig rosemary, for garnish

1. Combine the sugar, water, sea salt, and rosemary in a small saucepan. Heat over medium heat, stirring, until the sugar and salt are dissolved (no need to boil). Remove from the heat and let cool completely. Remove the rosemary and store the syrup in an airtight container in the fridge for up to a month.

2. To a cocktail shaker with no ice, add the gin, egg white, grapefruit juice, lemon juice, and simple syrup. Wrap a kitchen towel around the shaker and dry shake (without ice) for 20 seconds.

3. Add several ice cubes and shake until well chilled and frothy, about 20 seconds.

4. Strain into a coupe glass and top with club soda, if desired. Decorate the top with a few drops of bitters. Garnish with a citrus twist and a rosemary sprig and serve.

> **TIPS:** To use one whole egg white, double the other ingredients and make two drinks.
>
> You can use a pasteurized egg if you like, but the drink won't be quite as frothy.
>
> For a no-egg-white version, add all the ingredients except the soda to a shaker with ice and shake until cold. Strain into a collins glass filled with ice, top with soda, and garnish.
>
> The simple syrup will keep in an airtight container in the fridge for at least a month.

MAC: *"I hate gin! Get me a beer! Get me a beer!"*

DENNIS: *"Beer!"*

CHARLIE: *"Beer!"*

DEE: *"It's a gin bar!"*

GUIGINO'S $44 SNAPPER

If Guigino's famous snapper is sold out, skip the intermediary and make your own. Have the whole fish cleaned and prepped at the seafood counter for ease. It's an impressive, restaurant-worthy main dish that's incredibly simple to prepare.

Serves 2 · Prep Time: 10 minutes · Cook Time: 20 minutes

1 (2- to 3-pound) whole red snapper, cleaned and gutted

2 teaspoons olive oil

¾ teaspoon kosher salt, or to taste

½ teaspoon black pepper, or to taste

1 lemon, halved

3 garlic cloves, crushed and peeled

2 sprigs fresh thyme

1 sprig fresh rosemary

1 tablespoon butter, cut into quarters

1. Preheat the oven to 450°F. Line a rimmed baking sheet with foil.

2. Pat the fish dry with paper towels and place on the baking sheet. Coat inside and out with olive oil.

3. Season inside and outside generously with salt and pepper. Cut half the lemon into slices and stuff into the cavity. Cut the rest of the lemon into wedges and reserve for serving. Add the garlic and fresh herbs to the cavity with the lemon.

4. Bake the fish just until it is cooked through and flakes with a fork, about 20 minutes. Place the pieces of butter on top and let melt.

5. Serve immediately with lemon wedges.

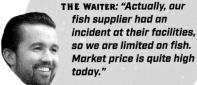

MAC: *"Get me the snapper, bozo."*

THE WAITER: *"Actually, our fish supplier had an incident at their facilities, so we are limited on fish. Market price is quite high today."*

MAC: *"Do you have the snapper or not?"*

ORGY SHRIMP COCKTAIL

You can't have an orgy without a good buffet, and you can't have a good buffet without shrimp cocktail. This recipe uses a simple poaching method that infuses the shrimp with flavor without overcooking it. The homemade cocktail sauce can be made a few days in advance and puts the appetizer over the top.

Serves 4 · Prep Time: 15 minutes · Cook Time: 3 minutes

2 lemons, quartered

Kosher or sea salt

1 pound (16 to 20) deveined, unpeeled shrimp

1 cup ketchup

2 tablespoons prepared horseradish

1 tablespoon lemon juice

½ teaspoon lemon zest

1 teaspoon Worcestershire sauce

½ teaspoon black pepper

1. Bring a medium-sized pot of water to a boil. Meanwhile, prepare an ice bath by adding cool water and ice cubes to a large bowl.

2. Squeeze the lemons into the boiling water and then toss in the quarters. Season the water generously with salt.

3. Remove the pot from the heat and add the shrimp. Let sit until the shrimp are cooked through, 2 to 3 minutes. Use a slotted spoon to transfer the cooked shrimp to the ice bath.

4. To make the sauce, add the ketchup, horseradish, lemon juice, lemon zest, Worcestershire sauce, and black pepper and stir to combine.

5. Once the shrimp are cooled, peel them, leaving the tails on, and pat dry. Serve alongside the sauce.

TIP: The cocktail sauce will keep in a sealed container in the fridge for a week.

DENNIS: *"Why is there a buffet at a goddamn orgy?"*

FRANK: *"You don't want to bang on an empty stomach!"*

THIN MINTS

If your cult leader doesn't allow you to eat Thin Mints (or it's not Girl Scout cookie season), make this homemade version. Be sure to chill the dough before slicing, and let the baked cookies cool completely on the baking sheet before coating in chocolate. Serve them cold, straight from the fridge.

Makes about 20 cookies · Prep Time: 20 minutes · Cook Time: 14 minutes

Chill Time: 30 minutes

½ cup unsalted butter, room temperature

¾ cup powdered sugar

1 teaspoon peppermint extract

¾ cup all-purpose flour

¼ cup Dutch-processed cocoa powder

¼ teaspoon salt

¾ cup chopped milk chocolate or milk chocolate chips

⅔ cup chopped semisweet or dark chocolate or chocolate chips

1 tablespoon refined coconut oil

1. Add the butter, powdered sugar, and peppermint extract to a medium-sized mixing bowl and beat together using an electric mixer until creamy, about 2 minutes. Add the flour, cocoa powder, and salt and beat until a soft dough forms.

2. Dump the dough out onto a piece of plastic wrap or wax paper. Form into a log about 1½ inches wide, rolling it back and forth to make a cylinder. Wrap tightly and refrigerate for at least 30 minutes.

3. Preheat the oven to 350°F. Line a baking sheet with parchment paper.

4. Unwrap the dough and slice into ⅜-inch slices. If it crumbles at all when slicing, use your hands to squeeze it back together. Place the slices at least 1 inch apart on the baking sheet.

5. Bake until the cookies are spread and set, 11 to 12 minutes. If you're baking two sheets at once, switch the sheets halfway through and bake for 12 to 13 total minutes. Let cool completely on the baking sheet.

6. Once the cookies have cooled, prepare a clean baking sheet by lining with a piece of parchment or wax paper and

(continued on next page)

[continued from previous page]

then placing a cooling rack on top. Combine the chocolate and coconut oil in a microwave-safe bowl. Microwave for 30-second increments, stirring after each time, until melted.

7. Place the cookies on the cooling rack spaced slightly apart. Spoon about a tablespoon of melted chocolate to the top of each cookie, spreading it gently in a circular pattern so that leaves a thin coating on the top and sides.

8. Gently tap the cooling rack a few times and let the excess chocolate drip through. Let the cookies sit until the chocolate sets up. If desired, transfer to the fridge to speed things up.

9. Any excess chocolate on the paper-lined baking sheet can be saved for another project. Store the cookies in an airtight container in the fridge for up to a week.

TIPS: Make sure to measure the flour properly or your dough will be too dry. Fluff it up, spoon it into a measuring cup so it rises above the top, and then sweep the excess off with the blunt side of a knife.

If you cut your cookies thicker, like ½ inch, cook them a minute or two longer.

DENNIS: *"I just made this shit up about Ass Kickers United to get Mac to stop eating my Thin Mints."*

CHARLIE: *"An Ass Kicker must avoid Thin Mints."*

MAC: *"I love these things."*

McPoyles' Milk Punch

Instead of spiking milk with bath salts, spike it with bourbon, brandy, amaretto, and a little simple syrup for a wedding-worthy cocktail. It's similar to eggnog without the eggs, making it a little less thick and rich and more suitable for year-round imbibing.

Serves 8 · Prep Time: 5 minutes · Cook Time: 0 minutes

2 cups whole milk

1 cup bourbon

½ cup brandy

¼ cup amaretto

⅓ cup simple syrup

Variation:

Swap the bourbon for dark rum.

1. Add the ingredients to a pitcher filled with ice. Stir until cold and strain into a small punch bowl. Serve.

TIPS: To make the simple syrup, combine 1 part granulated sugar with 1 part water in a small saucepan. Heat over medium heat, stirring, until the sugar dissolves. Cool, then transfer to a jar. Extra simple syrup will keep in the fridge for a month.

To make one drink, combine 2 ounces milk, 1 ounce bourbon, ½ ounce brandy, ¼ ounce amaretto, and ⅓ ounce simply syrup in a shaker with ice. Shake until cold, strain, and serve.

BILL PONDEROSA: *"It's a dry wedding, for god's sake. They're serving milk."*

BILL PONDEROSA: *"Here, have a sip right from the cow's titty. You'll love it."*

DEE: *"No, I gotta get out of here. Shit is going crazy."*

BILL PONDEROSA: *"No, don't go anywhere! The party's just starting. You gotta have some. Try it. It'll loosen you up a bit. Make your butthole hot!"*

"Mac"

HI, HYPERION, MAC AGAIN. *This is my third attempt to reach you. Why are you not responding to any of these? Please do not publish the book in this iteration. I do not consent to the photos you've used of me. I've since shredded down and built back with incredible lean muscle. I've even been told I look like a Greek god on multiple occasions. It was by the same person, and he was trying to get in my pants, but he said it twice.*

You'll recall I included photos of said sculpting in my previous correspondences. I even held up the day's Inquirer *to prove they are current and I'm not half-assing a pic from ten years ago like some washed-up jabroni on a dating app. However, much to my dismay, I see you have chosen not to swap out any of the pics from back when I was a shapeless blob. (That wasn't my fault, by the way; exercise science hadn't caught up to my opinions yet.)*

You'll also recall I was the one who pitched you this book, *shepherded you into Paddy's Pub, and gave you the trade secrets to the best recipes in this whole thing. (I mean, Fight Milk?! C'mon.) But I was clear that those invitations were extended only on the condition that you would showcase my Herculean physique, and not one—NOT ONE—photo of me in this draft properly depicts my awesome torso, tris, or bis. There's no other way to say it except that I feel exploited, and I will not do any press for this book until my demands are met.*

Also, thank you for working in the pear tart; I think Charlie's really going to like it.

FIGHT MILK

The original Fight Milk had some issues (diarrhea, vomiting, tons of growth hormones), so this version calls for chicken eggs instead of crow eggs. Use super-fresh eggs or pasteurized eggs since they're not cooked in this recipe. It's really just vodka eggnog—serve it for the holidays or any time you're itching for a fight.

Serves 4 · Prep Time: 12 minutes · Cook Time: 0 · Chill Time: 1 hour

4 eggs, separated

¼ cup plus 2 tablespoons sugar, divided

1 teaspoon vanilla extract

⅔ to ¾ cup vodka, to taste

2 cups whole milk

¾ cup heavy cream

Grated nutmeg, for garnish, optional

1. Combine the egg yolks, ¼ cup sugar, and vanilla in a small mixing bowl. Whisk until the sugar is dissolved and the mixture is pale yellow.

2. While whisking, slowly add the vodka. Then repeat with the milk and heavy cream.

3. Add the egg whites to a large mixing bowl and beat with a whisk or a hand mixer until doubled in volume and very frothy. Add the remaining 2 tablespoons sugar gradually while mixing. Beat until soft peaks form.

4. Whisk the egg whites into the egg yolk mixture.

5. Cover and chill for at least 1 hour or up to 24 hours before serving. Whisk to recombine just before serving. Garnish with grated nutmeg, if desired.

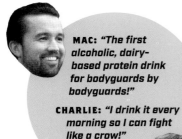

MAC: *"The first alcoholic, dairy-based protein drink for bodyguards by bodyguards!"*

CHARLIE: *"I drink it every morning so I can fight like a crow!"*

MAC: *"CAW!"*

Variations:

Swap the vodka for vanilla vodka and leave out the vanilla extract.

Replace the vodka with bourbon, brandy, or aged rum.

MAC'S FAMOUS MAC AND CHEESE

As easy to whip up as the blue-box stuff, this stove-top mac and cheese won't add any tension to your home life. A little cream cheese adds flavor and thickens the sauce without the need for a roux. Sharp cheddar is a classic choice, but use your favorite melty cheese.

Serves 6 · Prep Time: 5 minutes · Cook Time: 12 minutes

1 teaspoon salt plus more for the pasta water, divided

1 pound elbow macaroni

1½ cups whole milk

2 ounces cream cheese, room temperature, cubed

½ teaspoon garlic powder

3 cups shredded sharp cheddar cheese

DENNIS: *"Oh my god, Mac! This is incredible!"*

MAC: *"You like it? That's such a relief because I worked so hard on it. I call it Mac's Famous Mac and Cheese."*

1. Bring a big pot of water to a boil. Season generously with salt, add the macaroni, and stir. Cook until al dente according to the package directions. Drain.

2. Meanwhile, add the milk to a medium-sized saucepan and heat over medium heat.

3. Once the milk is beginning to steam, reduce the heat to low and add the cream cheese, 1 teaspoon salt, and garlic powder. Stir until smooth. Add half the shredded cheese and stir until melted, then add the rest of the cheese. Stir until smooth and creamy. Taste for seasoning.

4. Add the cooked and drained macaroni to a large serving dish or the empty pasta pot. Add the sauce and stir until well coated. The sauce will thicken as it cools. Serve immediately.

Variation:

If you want to mix things up, add meat chunks (chopped ham).

HOBO BEANS

You don't need to be a hobo to enjoy baked beans. Thanks to the inclusion of ground beef and bacon, it's practically a meal all on its own. Use your favorite barbecue sauce and your choice of canned beans.

Serves 8 · Prep Time: 10 minutes · Cook Time: 90 minutes

6 slices bacon, diced

1 onion, diced

1 small bell pepper, diced

1 pound lean ground beef

2 garlic cloves, minced

1 (15-ounce) can pinto beans, rinsed and drained

1 (15-ounce) can kidney beans, rinsed and drained

1 (15-ounce) can lima beans or navy beans, rinsed and drained

½ cup barbecue sauce

½ cup ketchup

⅓ cup brown sugar, packed

3 tablespoons apple cider vinegar

2 teaspoons smoked paprika

2 teaspoons dry mustard or Dijon mustard

½ teaspoon kosher salt

1. Preheat the oven to 325°F. Add the bacon to a large, heavy-bottomed pot with a lid (like a Dutch oven) and heat, uncovered, over medium heat. Cook, stirring occasionally, until lightly crisp. Remove the bacon to a paper towel–lined plate, but reserve the bacon grease.

2. Add the onion and bell pepper to the bacon fat and sauté until the onion begins to turn translucent, about 4 minutes. Add the ground beef and garlic. Cook, breaking up the meat with a wooden spoon, until the beef is browned. Turn off the heat and use a spoon to scoop out most of the fat.

3. Add the pinto, kidney, and lima or navy beans and stir. Add the barbecue sauce, ketchup, brown sugar, vinegar, smoked paprika, mustard, and salt and stir well to coat. Top with the bacon and cover with the lid.

4. Transfer the Dutch oven to the preheated oven and bake until bubbly, 35 to 45 minutes. Remove the lid and cook until thick, about 30 more minutes. Let sit about 10 minutes before serving.

Variation:

Use any combination of pinto, kidney, navy, white northern, cannellini, and lima beans.

CHARLIE: *"We should have gotten beans, dude! Hobos are always eating beans."*

MAC: *"We'll be fine without the beans, all right? Because this is a perfect, perfect hiding spot."*

CHARLIE: *"This would be better with beans, though."*

PEAR TART FOR CHARLIE

If you have a friend who's never tried a pear or blueberries, ease them into the wide world of fruit with this lovely tart. The crust comes together quickly and doesn't need to be prebaked, and the filling is a simple layer of blueberries topped with sliced pear and flavored with lemon, brown sugar, and a touch of cinnamon.

Makes one 9-inch tart · Prep Time: 30 minutes · Cook Time: 40 minutes

Chill Time: 30 minutes · Cool Time: 2 hours

FOR THE CRUST:

1¼ cups all-purpose flour

2 tablespoons cornstarch

1 tablespoon sugar

½ teaspoon kosher salt

6 tablespoons unsalted butter, cubed

1 egg, lightly beaten

FOR THE FILLING:

3 medium-sized pears

2 tablespoons fresh lemon juice

¼ cup brown sugar, packed

1½ tablespoons cornstarch

½ teaspoon cinnamon

¼ teaspoon kosher salt

6 ounces fresh blueberries

1 tablespoon honey

½ teaspoon hot water

1. Add the flour, cornstarch, sugar, and salt to a medium-sized mixing bowl. Add the butter and toss with the flour. Use your fingers to rub the butter into the flour until all the pieces of butter are pea-sized or smaller. The mixture should look like clumpy cornmeal.

2. Add the egg and use a spatula to mix. Use your hands to press the mixture together, turning and pressing until a dough forms. Transfer to a lightly floured surface and form the dough into a disk.

3. Use a rolling pin to roll the dough into a 12-inch circle, rotating to keep it from sticking and adding sprinkles of flour if needed. If the dough splits at the edges, press it back together with your hands.

(continued on next page)

CHARLIE: *"I've never eaten a pear."*

MAC: *"What?! How is that possible?"*

CHARLIE: *"Pears weird me out, dude. Where do you start with a pear? The top? The bottom?"*

(continued from previous page)

4. Drape the dough over a 9-inch tart pan and lift and press it into the corners and ridges, trimming any excess. Place the lined pan in the fridge and chill for 30 minutes. Preheat the oven to 375°F and arrange an oven rack in the bottom third of the oven.

5. Meanwhile, peel and core the pears, and then cut them into ½-inch slices. Add to a large mixing bowl and toss with the lemon juice.

6. In a small bowl, combine the brown sugar, cornstarch, cinnamon, and salt. Add all but roughly 1 tablespoon of this sugar mixture to the cut pears and toss well to coat.

7. Add the blueberries to the chilled piecrust in an even layer and sprinkle with the remaining sugar mixture. Arrange the pear slices on top, and then coat with any remaining syrup scraped from the bowl.

8. Bake until the berries are bubbly, the pears are tender, and the crust is golden brown, 40 to 45 minutes.

9. Let the tart cool for a few minutes, and combine the honey and hot water in a small bowl. Brush the mixture on top of the tart. Let cool completely (at least 2 hours) before serving.

CHARLIE: *"Hey, I've never had blueberries, either."*

TRASH CAN "MICROBREW"

You're sure to be the star of the bar crawl with this boozy shandy. The combination of lemonade, moonshine, and beer couldn't be easier and is super refreshing on a hot day. Make your own lemonade with fresh lemons for a superior drink.

Serves 1 · Prep Time: 5 minutes · Cook Time: 0 minutes

2 ounces lemonade

1 ounce moonshine

3 ounces pale ale or other light, crisp beer

1. Combine the lemonade and moonshine in a beer glass. Stir and fill with ice.

2. Top with the beer and give the drink a gentle stir. Serve.

TIPS: Plain or citrus-flavored moonshine works best.

A light, crisp, and refreshing (not-too-hoppy) beer is a good fit for a shandy like this one. Pale ales, easy-drinking pilsners, not-too-heavy wheat ales, and light beers are all good choices.

If your lemonade is on the weak side, add an extra ounce, or to taste.

To make a quick lemonade, combine 1 part fresh lemon juice with 1 part granulated sugar and 6 parts water. Stir until the sugar is completely dissolved.

MAC: *"That's enough moonshine, Frank! We don't want people to go blind!"*

FRANK: *"You can never have enough moonshine!"*

CONFESSIONAL DOUGHNUTS

Confess your sins (such as gluttony) while eating these shortcut doughnuts. Instead of mixing up homemade dough, rolling it out, and waiting for it to rise, use store-bought canned biscuit dough instead. Simply cut a hole, fry, and glaze.

Makes 8 doughnuts plus holes · Prep Time: 15 minutes · Cook Time: 15 minutes

1 to 2 quarts canola or vegetable oil

1 (16-ounce) can biscuits, not flaky

1 cup powdered sugar

1 teaspoon vanilla

⅛ teaspoon salt

⅛ teaspoon nutmeg

2 to 4 tablespoons milk

Food coloring, optional

Sprinkles, optional

TIPS: If you don't have a 1-inch cutter, look for a screw top. Many liquor bottles and twist-off wine bottles have roughly 1-inch tops.

If your glaze ends up too thin, add more powdered sugar. You want it to coat the doughnuts easily without dripping too much.

1. Add enough oil to a heavy-bottomed, large pot with high sides to reach 1 inch up the side. Heat on medium heat to 350°F. Line a baking sheet with paper towels.

2. Meanwhile, open the canned biscuits and separate them, laying them flat on a clean work surface. Use a 1-inch circle-shaped cutter to make center holes in each, reserving the extra dough to make doughnut holes.

3. Once the oil is hot, add 3 or 4 doughnuts to the oil, being careful to not overcrowd the pan. Fry until a deep golden brown, about 2 to 3 minutes, then flip and fry on the other side, about 2 to 3 minutes more.

4. Use a spider or slotted spoon to remove the doughnuts from the oil, and place them on the lined baking sheet. Let the oil come back to temperature and repeat with the remaining doughnuts.

5. After all the doughnuts are fried, add the doughnut holes and cook until golden brown while flipping periodically, 2 to 3 minutes.

6. To make the glaze, combine the powdered sugar, vanilla, salt, and nutmeg in a small mixing bowl. Add 2 tablespoons of milk and whisk together, adding more milk 1 teaspoon at a time until you reach the right consistency for dipping. Add food coloring, if desired, and stir to combine.

7. Dip each doughnut in the glaze, letting the excess drip off. Place back on the lined baking sheet. If desired, decorate with sprinkles while the glaze is still wet. Let the glaze set for several minutes, then serve.

TRASH BAG FULL OF CHIMICHANGAS

If you're feeding a crowd (or one Mac) or want to do some meal prep, this batch chimichanga recipe is the solution. They're easy to assemble and they bake in the oven instead of frying, making for simpler clean-up.

Serves 8 · Prep Time: 15 minutes · Cook Time: 15 minutes

- 4 tablespoons canola or vegetable oil, divided
- 4 cups cooked, shredded beef, pork, or chicken
- 1 (14-ounce) can fire-roasted diced tomatoes, drained
- 1 (4-ounce) can green chiles, drained
- 1 (1-ounce) taco seasoning packet
- 8 (10- or 12-inch) flour tortillas
- 2 (15-ounce) cans pinto beans, rinsed and drained
- 2 cups shredded Monterey Jack or cheddar cheese
- 1 cup thin red or green salsa or enchilada sauce
- ½ cup sour cream

1. Preheat the oven to 450°F. Brush a large rimmed baking sheet with an even coating of 2 to 3 tablespoons of oil.

2. Combine the shredded meat, canned tomatoes, chiles, and taco seasoning in a mixing bowl and stir.

3. Add a heaping ½ cup of the mixture to the center of a tortilla, making a 6-inch line in the center. Add a heaping ¼ cup of beans in a line next to the meat mixture. Top with ¼ cup shredded cheese.

4. Fold in the edges of the tortilla on each end of the line of filling. Roll up in the opposite direction into a burrito. Repeat with the remaining tortillas and fillings.

5. Place them seam-side down on the oiled baking sheet. Brush the tops and sides with the remaining oil.

6. Bake until beginning to brown on the top, 6 to 10 minutes. Brush the tops of the chimichangas with some oil from the pan and continue baking until browned, 4 to 8 more minutes.

7. Serve topped with salsa or enchilada sauce and a dollop of sour cream.

DENNIS: *"You are becoming a chimichanga!"*

> **TIP:** Halve this recipe to serve 4 using a quarter sheet pan; or you can just use the large rimmed baking sheet. For the halved recipe, decrease the oil to 3 tablespoons total (2 to oil the baking sheet and 1 to brush on top of the chimichangas).

MAC'S CHIPS

Homemade potato chips are so good that you'll be hogging them all for yourself just like Mac. There are a few keys to success: slice the potatoes very thin (a mandolin or food processor with a slicer attachment is best for this), give them a good wash in cool water, and dry them extremely well before frying.

Serves 6 · Prep Time: 20 minutes · Cook Time: 15 minutes

1 pound russet potatoes

2 quarts canola or vegetable oil, or as needed

Salt, to taste

CHARLIE: *"Dude, please give me a chip."*

MAC: *"Leave me alone with the chips! If you wanted chips, you should have gotten a bag at the hamburger store!"*

1. Peel and slice the potatoes ⅛ inch thick using a mandoline or a food processor with a slicing attachment.

2. Add the sliced potatoes to a large bowl and cover with cool water. Use your hands to swish the potato slices in the water, helping them to release their starch. Repeat a few times, draining the water and replacing it with clean water, until the water is mostly clear.

3. Drain the potatoes. Lay them out in a single layer on a large, clean kitchen towel or paper towels and pat dry. You may have to work in batches.

4. Add enough oil to a large, heavy-bottomed skillet with tall sides to reach 1 inch up the sides. Heat over medium heat to 350°F. Line a baking sheet with paper towels.

5. Add a third of the chips, a handful at a time, to the hot oil. Stir to separate. Fry, stirring often, until crisp and lightly golden, with some chips turning brown in spots, about 5 minutes.

6. Remove the chips with a slotted spoon or spider and transfer to the lined baking sheet. Immediately sprinkle with salt. Let the oil come back to temperature, then repeat with the remaining batches of potato. Cool and serve.

> **TIP:** Be sure to use a big, heavy-bottomed skillet with high sides. Don't add too many slices of potato at one time, since the oil will boil up after each addition and could boil over.

FRANK: *"This is a much better spread than they have at the straight orgies."*

SEX DUNGEON BUFFALO WINGS

Buffalo wings are a favorite appetizer suited to almost any occasion, from game days to sex parties. This recipe is a small batch made using an air fryer, so you don't even need an excuse to whip some up. Don't forget the blue cheese or ranch dressing for dipping.

Serves 1 to 2 · Prep Time: 10 minutes · Cook Time: 30 minutes · Chill Time: 1 hour

1 pound chicken wings (trimmed, without drumettes and tips)

¼ teaspoon kosher salt, plus a pinch for the sauce

¼ teaspoon black pepper

¼ teaspoon garlic powder

Nonstick cooking spray

3 tablespoons hot sauce

3 tablespoons unsalted butter, melted

2 celery ribs, cut into sticks

1 carrot, peeled and cut into sticks

Blue cheese or ranch dressing, for serving

1. Pat the wings dry with a paper towel. Place on a plate lined with a clean paper towel and transfer to the fridge, uncovered. Let chill for at least 1 hour or up to 8 hours.

2. Preheat the air fryer to 360°F. Combine the salt, pepper, and garlic powder in a small bowl. Season the chicken on all sides.

3. Spray the air fryer basket with nonstick cooking spray. Add the wings in a single layer and spray lightly with cooking spray. Replace the basket.

4. Cook for 12 to 13 minutes, flip the wings, and cook for 11 to 13 more minutes. Flip again and increase the temperature to 400°F. Cook until crispy, 5 to 10 minutes.

5. Meanwhile, add the hot sauce, melted butter, and a pinch of salt to a medium-sized bowl and whisk.

6. Add the cooked wings to the sauce and toss to coat. Serve immediately with celery, carrot, and blue cheese or ranch dressing on the side.

FRANK: *"Ooh, spicy. There must be some hot sauce on those wings."*

MAC: *"They're buffalo wings!"*

TIPS: It's easy to double this recipe to make 2 pounds of wings. If you have a small air fryer, cook them in 2 batches.

If you don't have an air fryer, you can bake them instead. Coat the chilled chicken wings in a small amount of oil and sprinkle with seasoning. Place on a wire rack on top of a rimmed baking sheet and bake at 425°F until crisp, about 45 minutes, flipping halfway. Toss in the sauce.

CRICKET'S DANCE MARATHON ENERGY BARS

If you're feeling a bit sluggish, try a Cricket's Dance Marathon Energy Bar. More of a brownie-meets-cookie than a bar, the soft, chewy mounds are packed with energizing chocolate and coffee. Skip the cough medicine unless you're looking to sabotage the competition.

Makes 8 · Prep Time: 15 minutes · Cook Time: 12 minutes

- 1⅔ cups all-purpose flour
- ⅓ cup Dutch-processed cocoa powder
- 2 teaspoons baking powder
- ¾ teaspoon salt
- 10 tablespoons unsalted butter or vegan butter, melted
- ⅔ cup brown sugar, packed
- ⅓ cup sugar
- ¼ cup brewed coffee (any variety), room temperature
- 1 teaspoon vanilla extract
- 4 ounces semisweet or dark chocolate bar, divided into ½-ounce squares

FRANK: *"We're making brownies."*

CRICKET: *"The drug-filled kind!"*

FRANK: *"Shut up, Cricket!"*

DEE: *"Looks like a shit ball."*

1. Preheat the oven to 350°F. Line a large baking sheet with parchment paper.

2. In a medium-sized mixing bowl, combine the flour, cocoa powder, baking powder, and salt. Whisk to completely combine and break up any lumps.

3. In a separate large bowl, combine the melted butter, brown sugar, and sugar. Whisk for 1 minute. Add the coffee and vanilla and whisk to combine.

4. Add the dry ingredients to the wet ingredients. Use a wooden spoon or rubber spatula to mix just until completely combined.

5. Measure out ¼ cup of dough. If the dough is too soft to work with, place it in the fridge for 15 to 30 minutes. Press a ½-ounce square of chocolate in the middle and form the dough around it, creating a mound about 2½ to 3 inches wide with chocolate in the center. Place on the baking sheet.

6. Repeat with the remaining dough and chocolate, spacing the balls at least 2 inches apart.

7. Bake until puffed and no longer shiny, 12 to 15 minutes. Let cool for several minutes on the baking sheet. Serve warm.

"Dee"

DID THAT SOY BOY EDITOR say I wasn't a big-time actress? Mmmkay, buddy. Let's see how many "Obnoxious American MILF" credits you have on your IMDb. Anyways. Sorry to come in hot like that, but for all those familiar with my onstage work, you already know ya girl's not going to sit and get heckled without blasting back a few well-timed wallops of her own. And for those not yet familiar with my work, I'll direct you to find me on TikTok, where I'm whipping up bar and kitchen masterpieces—and zingers—just like these on the reg. So, come on in and join the action. Just like you are hungry reading this book—or at least this section—mama is hungry for those likes and subscribes, so help me out here. Just don't enter the kitchen if you can't handle the heat!

When I heard they were sticking my section at the end, I scoffed, but then I realized they were saving the best for last. Obviously. I mean, who isn't waiting for all the cocktails? (And who doesn't need one after those last four sections, amirite?) Luckily, you've come to the right place, and I have many a cure for what ails you. I've picked up a thing or two in my time bartending at Paddy's—and no, I don't just mean scruffy stragglers hot off a divorce. Getting the finest of Philadelphia drunk has shown me that when it comes to boozin', the more signature the cocktail, the more signatures you get on bills. Know what I'm sayin'? The more MOOLAH you make. Not that we're making any off this, unfortunately. But it is exposure and audience-building, which to some is more valuable than money. Although money is nice, too, and my tricks will definitely make you money.

So, use these barside favorites of mine to pay for your next improv class. And if they don't, just double drop the check. That's always worked for me.

COSMOPOLITAN

No ladies' night is complete without a cosmo! The classic drink balances tart, sweet, and boozy flavors for a well-rounded, pink-hued drink. You can use citrus vodka instead or adjust the ratios to suit your tastes.

Makes 1 drink · Prep Time: 5 minutes · Cook Time: 0 minutes

2 ounces vodka

¾ ounce Cointreau

¾ ounce cranberry juice cocktail

½ ounce fresh lime juice

1 orange twist, for garnish, optional

1. Combine the vodka, Cointreau, cranberry juice, and lime juice in a shaker filled with ice. Shake until cold, about 20 seconds.

2. Strain into a chilled martini or coupe glass. Garnish with an orange twist and serve.

Variations:

For a fruitier cosmo, use 1 ounce cranberry juice or swap the Cointreau for triple sec.

Swap the vodka for citron vodka.

DEE: *"She'll take a cosmo, and she'll just hold it in her hand."*

ARTEMIS: *"I have a bleached asshole!"*

PADDY'S PUB SNACK MIX

Every good bar needs a snack mix, and this lightly spicy, salty mix will have customers ordering beer after beer. For a no-nut version, replace the peanuts with more cereal, pretzels, and/or crackers. If you're really into spice, add extra hot sauce.

Makes 8 cups · Prep Time: 10 minutes · Cook Time: 45 minutes

4 tablespoons unsalted butter

1 tablespoon Worcestershire sauce

2 to 3 teaspoons Louisiana hot sauce, to taste

2 teaspoons Creole or Cajun seasoning

3 cups Corn Chex

2 cups pretzels

2 cups Cheez-It crackers

1 cup salted peanuts

1. Preheat the oven to 250°F.

2. Add the butter, Worcestershire sauce, hot sauce, and seasoning to a microwave-safe bowl. Microwave in 30-second increments until the butter has melted, stirring to combine.

3. Add the cereal, pretzels, cheese crackers, and peanuts to a large rimmed baking sheet. Top with the butter mixture and toss well to completely coat.

4. Spread into an even layer and bake for 45 minutes, stirring every 15 minutes. Let cool and store in an airtight container.

FRANK: *"Don't you guys get tired of doing nothin' except sitting around drinkin'?"*

DENNIS: *"How could you ever get tired of that? I don't understand."*

DEE: *"Is that a joke?"*

HEALTH JUICE

This combination of green vegetables, herbs, and fruit is sure to cure whatever ails you, even if that sickness is just caring for your child. While it's best made with a juicer, you can whirl everything up in a blender and strain it for a healthy, bright green juice.

Serves 2 · Prep Time: 10 minutes · Cook Time: 0 minutes

1 medium-sized cucumber

2 celery ribs

3 to 4 large kale leaves

4 sprigs fresh mint

1 cup pineapple chunks

1 lemon

1 (1-inch) piece fresh ginger

1. Add all the ingredients to a juicer, trimming and chopping as needed to fit, and juice. Alternatively, add everything but the lemon to a blender. Halve the lemon, squeeze the lemon juice into the blender, and process until smooth.

2. If using the blender method (or if you prefer a thinner juice), strain through a fine-mesh strainer, using a spoon to press the mixture through the strainer.

DEE: *"I feel like that green stuff is really working."*

FRANK: *"The bitch is driving me crazy! She's not even sick anymore!"*

PHILLY CHEESESTEAKS

Take a trip to Philly without ever leaving home by making homemade Philly Cheesesteaks. Freeze the steak for 20 minutes to make it easier to cut into thin slices that cook quickly and crisp in the pan. The recipe yields two large cheesesteaks or three medium-sized sandwiches that will make you want to eat like a giant bird.

Serves 2 to 3 · Prep Time: 10 minutes · Cook Time: 15 minutes · Freeze Time: 20 minutes

1 pound boneless ribeye steak

¾ teaspoon salt, divided

½ teaspoon pepper, divided

1 tablespoon plus 1 teaspoon canola oil, divided

½ large sweet onion, thinly sliced

1 green bell pepper, thinly sliced

2 to 3 hoagie rolls

2 tablespoons butter, softened

½ teaspoon garlic powder

4 ounces sliced or shredded provolone cheese or Cheez Whiz

Variation:

For an extra-cheesy cheesesteak, put the provolone on the bottom followed by the steak and peppers and add Cheez Whiz on top.

CHARLIE: *"Dee, will you calm down? You're eating that cheesesteak like some kind of giant bird."*

DEE: *"I can't help it, Charlie! I've got an insatiable hunger."*

1. Place the steak in the freezer for 20 minutes. Trim any large pieces of fat and slice into very thin slices against the grain. Season with half the salt and pepper.

2. Add 1 tablespoon of canola oil to a medium-sized skillet over medium heat. Add the onion and green pepper and cook, stirring occasionally, until tender and lightly browned, about 10 minutes. Season with the remaining salt and pepper.

3. Use a serrated knife to cut the hoagie rolls almost in half, leaving attached at one end so you can open them like a book. Combine the butter and garlic powder in a small bowl and spread on the inside of each roll.

4. Heat a large skillet (preferably cast-iron) or griddle over medium-high heat. Add the remaining teaspoon of oil followed by the steak. Spread out into a single layer and let brown until and mostly cooked through, then flip and cook until cooked through and crisp on the outside, about 3 minutes total.

5. Meanwhile, add the hoagie rolls to the griddle, cut side down, and lightly toast, about a minute. Alternatively, broil for a few minutes, cut side up.

6. Add the onions and peppers to the steak and toss to combine, warming everything through. Distribute among the toasted rolls and immediately top with the cheese. If needed, broil the hoagies just until the cheese is melted.

DEE'S MOJITO

Whether you're trying to prove you're a good bartender or just want to enjoy a refreshing beverage, a mojito is the answer. Instead of requiring a muddler, this recipe lets you get your frustrations out with a good shake. Two kinds of rum make it twice as good.

Makes 1 cocktail · Prep Time: 8 minutes · Cook Time: 0 minutes

6 fresh mint leaves

2 teaspoons sugar

1 ounce fresh lime juice

1½ ounces white rum

1 ounce aged rum

2 ounces club soda, or to taste

1 mint sprig, for garnish

1 lime wedge, for garnish

1. Add the mint leaves, sugar, and lime juice to a cocktail shaker or jar. Add 2 ice cubes and close the lid.

2. Shake vigorously until all the sugar has dissolved and the mint has broken up, 30 seconds to 1 minute.

3. Strain into a collins glass and top with ice.

4. Add both of the rums and the club soda and stir. Garnish with mint and lime and serve.

Variations:

Use all white or all aged rum.

Swap the rum for vodka.

DEE: *"Nobody orders a mojito in this bar."*

DENNIS: *"So you can't make a mojito?"*

DEE: *"Fine, one mojito coming up, gentlemen! . . . I quit."*

RIOT JUICE

When you want to get crazy at the big game, nothing will do but grain alcohol. If you're a lightweight, swap it for vodka instead. Blue curaçao adds sweetness and gives the drink its signature color.

Makes 1 drink · Prep Time: 5 minutes · Cook Time: 0 minutes

1½ ounces grain alcohol, like Everclear

¾ ounce fresh lime juice

½ ounce blue curaçao

3 to 4 ounces lemon-lime soda, or to taste

1. In a collins glass or other tall glass, combine the grain alcohol, lime juice, and blue curaçao. Add ice and stir until cold, about 20 seconds.

2. Top with the lemon-lime soda to taste and gently stir. Add more ice, if needed, and serve.

Variation:

Swap the grain alcohol for vodka or white rum and increase to 2 ounces.

DENNIS: *"I'm not going to be cold at all. I'm going to be wasted on grain alcohol."*

MAC: *"Grain alcohol, baby! Whenever there is a potential riot, I'm going to be wasted on grain alcohol."*

TRASH CAKE

No one will be tossing this buttermilk-lemon cake with cream cheese frosting in the trash. It's just too good. You can bake the cake as two 8-inch layers or three 6-inch layers, depending on how tall you'd like your finished cake to be.

Makes one 2- or 3-layer cake · Prep Time: 30 minutes · Cook Time: 30 minutes

Cool Time: 1 hour

FOR THE CAKE:

- 1 cup unsalted butter, room temperature
- 1½ cups sugar
- 3 large eggs, room temperature
- 1 tablespoon lemon zest
- 1 teaspoon vanilla extract
- 2¾ cups all-purpose flour
- 2 teaspoons baking powder
- ½ teaspoon baking soda
- 1 teaspoon salt
- 1 cup plus 1 tablespoon buttermilk, room temperature
- ⅓ cup lemon juice

FOR THE FROSTING:

- 16 ounces (2 packs) cream cheese, room temperature
- 1 cup unsalted butter, room temperature
- 2 teaspoons lemon zest
- 2 teaspoon vanilla extract
- ¼ teaspoon salt
- 5 to 6 cups powdered sugar, sifted

1. Preheat the oven to 325°F. Spray two 8-inch or three 6-inch round cake pans with cooking spray and line the bottoms with circles of parchment paper.

2. To make the cakes, add the butter and sugar to the bowl of a stand mixer or a large mixing bowl. Beat on medium speed until fluffy, about 2 minutes. Add the eggs, one at a time, beating after each. Add the zest and vanilla and beat to combine. Scrape down the sides.

3. In a separate mixing bowl, sift together the flour, baking powder, baking soda, and salt.

4. With the mixer running on low, slowly add the flour mixture and combine. Add the buttermilk and lemon juice and mix on low until combined, scraping down the sides and bottoms of the bowl as needed.

5. Divide the batter evenly between the pans. Bake until the edges are golden, a toothpick inserted in the center comes out clean, and the top of the cake springs back when gently pressed: 25 to 32 minutes for three 6-inch pans or 28 to 36 minutes for two 8-inch pans.

6. Let the cakes cool in their pans for about 10 minutes before turning them out onto a cooling rack and cooling completely.

(continued on next page)

(continued from previous page)

7. To make the frosting, combine the cream cheese and butter in the bowl of a stand mixer or a large mixing bowl. Beat on medium speed until fluffy, about 3 minutes. Add the zest, vanilla, and salt and beat to combine.

8. Slowly add 5 cups of powdered sugar and beat until smooth and creamy. If desired, add more powdered sugar for a stiffer, sweeter frosting.

9. Frost the cake, building up one layer at a time with frosting in between. Use the remaining frosting to coat the top and sides. Cover the cake and store it in the fridge, removing it about 20 minutes before slicing and serving.

TIPS: For a light and fluffy cake, measure your flour properly. Fluff the flour in the container or bag, then spoon it into a measuring cup so it is higher than the sides. Use the straight edge of a butter knife to sweep away the excess flour, creating a level top. And don't skip the sifting step.

If you don't have buttermilk, use a mixture of ¾ cup plain yogurt and ¼ cup plus 1 tablespoon milk.

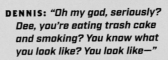

CHARLIE: *"That's Frank's cake from, like, a month ago. I threw that in the trash."*

DENNIS: *"Oh my god, seriously? Dee, you're eating trash cake and smoking? You know what you look like? You look like—"*

DEE: *"Like a bird? Like a bird lady covered in bird shit eating cake?"*

BLUE HOLE

Brightly colored and tropical, the Blue Hole is sure to become your signature drink and win an award among your friends. Tequila is swapped for rum for a different take on a tiki-style drink, but silver rum is also a good choice if you're not a tequila fan. Don't skimp on the garnishes.

Serves 3 · Prep Time: 8 minutes · Cook Time: 0 minutes

4 ounces blanco tequila

4 ounces pineapple juice

1½ to 2 ounces blue curaçao

1½ ounces fresh lime juice

½ ounce orgeat, optional

1 orange slice, for garnish

Fresh pineapple wedges and leaves, for garnish

Extra-long toothpick, for garnish

1 miniature umbrella, for garnish

3 boba straws, for serving

1. Combine the tequila, pineapple juice, 1½ ounces blue curaçao, lime juice, and orgeat (if using) in a pitcher filled with ice. Stir until very cold, about 20 seconds. If the mixture isn't blue enough, add another ½ ounce curaçao.

2. Ladle into a large glass or small fishbowl, adding more ice as needed. Lay the orange slice on top.

3. Thread a couple of fresh pineapple wedges and a few leaves onto an extra-long toothpick. Stick the umbrella in the side of a pineapple wedge and balance the whole thing on the rim of the glass. Add boba straws and serve.

BARTENDER: *"So one Blue Hole?"*

DENNIS: *"Uhh, well, let's see, so there's three of us, so three drinks."*

BARTENDER: *"Well, they're generally shared because they're pretty big—"*

DEE: *"I said three, dickbag!"*

MAC: *"GET THREE!"*